ASSORTED CHUNKS

SWARNIM WAINGANKAR

Contents

Preface

To all those who are interested and not-so-interested in poetry, this book will connect to you with its simplest words, not at all testing your vocabulary as you might have experienced in other poetic pieces.

This book is more of the emotional and social quotient. It is about considering your sentiments, people, experiences and things around you a bit more than usual... If we have no option other than going through the highs and lows that are thrown on us daily, why not feel them completely and move forward? We try to control our emotions (whether good or bad) so often, that we forget to live them fully and they get bottled up to burst out even greater someday. Express more often, appreciate a bit more, be patient with yourself and others, celebrate the silliest things, cry out loud when sad, allow to feel and absorb whatever comes to you!

Developing emotional stability is as important as evolving practical ability.

'Assorted Chunks' is a collection of those 18 times, when life wonderfully or sadly interrupted my psyche and I was able to pen it down!

Hope these chunks leave you with a pleasant aftertaste!

1. In my dreams...

Just wandered into my dreams last night,
Gazing through the secret of lovliest sight.
And thought this fantasy I'd let all know,
Glad that my soul knew where to go !

It wasnt about the castle of cake,
Not even the icy and creamy lake.
Neither about the huge toffee town,
Nor seeking the treasured shiny crown.

I dreamt of such a wonderland ,
Showering love with my magic wand.
Upon that kindness shall mercy dwell,
Ruled by a Fairy's mysterious spell !

I dreamt of stepping into others' shoe,
To feel all the pain that they alone do.
A land where we drink the words we waste,
Only to realize how bitter those taste !

I dreamt of a land without hatred and lie,
Where people are sweeter than the choco-pie !

A land having no sorrows of death,
Neither last wish nor last breath.

My delusion of this 'castle in the air',
Where everything seemed so right and fair.
Was soon to end its fancy delight,
As it vanished in the dawn's early light !

2. The display picture.

Aren't we spinning much, over this social-media culture,
We jump onto guesses, just from the display picture!

Do not be fooled by that false happy show,
No one is updating about their deepest low.

Instagram today, feels like a marriage race,
We are still free to run, at our very own pace.

Oh don't be jealous of the trips they afford
Even your fun-breaks are soon on the board !

Hell of efforts behind, but who gives a fuck?
There's more to the success story than sheer luck!

Is the facebook going to decide who likes you?
Believe me folks, ya'll dont need a review!

Since nobody is posting their failed venture,
You're much more than your display picture!

3. The old-school love

Love is not those plenty hours of talking, its when unanswered calls make you worry about that person..

Love is not when you think you would die without them, its when you believe that living with them is a blessing..

Love is not when you are fearless to odds bcoz you are with them, its when losing them is the only thing you fear..

Love is not when someone keeps all their promises,its when they deliver more than they had promised..

Love is not when you can share comfortable silence,its when you unstopably express all the feelings in words..

Love is not when you always think of someone, its when no other thought pops up while you think of them..

Love is not when someone makes you smile all the time,its when they are the only ones who can stop you from crying..

Love is not when you count the time,gifts,money that you

spend on someone,its when you realize that they are worth everything..!

4. Golden age

"Granny! Grandpa!" you ran through all their house,
The excitement you had then, does that still arouse?

Now those feelings; are nowhere to be seen,
No love from the child; only grandies are keen.

You dump them rudely; to the old-age-care,
Oldies living with their children; seems so rare.

No one protects you; and loves you like them,
You grew into a flower; on their caring stem.

They forget, they fumble; but so did you,
They were very patient; while you were new!

Sometimes they cribb; but console their scar,
Treat them lovingly, as special as they are!

Depart them in peace and adorn their last page
I promise you'll be loved then, in your golden-age!

5. Looking at the flipside..

When mom was hospitalized
In the peak Covid-wave,
The reports said positive
We prayed as hell to save

On those sleepless nights,
All were tensed too much,
As the condition worsened
We hoped for a divine touch.

No one could stay with her
Was indeed the worst part,
Food stuck in her throat
And fear in our heart.

Looking at the flipside I feel
Her health was soon mending,
We were thankful that she was back
Since so many hugs were pending

Finally turned out good
A really exhausting chapter,
We smiled with teary eyes

It was to be our 'happily ever after'...

6. Odd man out

Rushed into a trainee's job
Thats all it was about,
But among the fellows there
I was certainly an 'odd man out'

Hobbies, food and movies
Nothing could match, was the cause,
I stood up for a disliked opinion
Such a misfit I was!

I was the topic of their gossip
They admired what I hated,
Called me a moron instead
Coz ,"I dont drink" is what I said !

Why couldnt they respect
The (afterall) personal choices,
I was literally forced to shut up
By all those unworthy voices..

Would you prefer a crowd
Where hardly anybody cares,

So by this time now
I did not want to be theirs..

They got none of what I had
My heart used to shout,
From that onwards I realised
its okay being an 'odd man out'

Trolled and teased than ever
I literally lost all my charm,
Soon I had to get it back
As It was a self-worth alarm!

Alone but happier in my aura
I emptied all the self-doubt,
And for the first time ever
I loved being an 'odd man out' !

7. Listen up!

Somedays we just need someone who listens.
No suggestions,
No opinions,
No judgements.

Someone who just listens
to know, to understand.

People dont need any reviews, encouragement or consolation. They need an ear who attends their complaints, their regrets, joys, efforts, and feelings bottled up within.

Sometimes being a good listener is as important as being a good responder!

8. Goodbyes

Goodbyes are so difficult for me
Sad, unpleasant faces to see,
Recalling the past days of glee
Someday together hoping to be !

Though at every start I knew
Memories stay and bonding blew,
Still I thought I can make it through
But Indeed hard was to bid adieu...

No matter how hard I try
I cant smile and wave a bye,
I wish this farewell could be a lie
But all is real and makes me cry..

I want some people to stay forever
Also moments that wont return ever,
Thats something I cant get over
Still cheerless in the same hangover!

Drowned in the deep memory-sea
Though it wont last long I agree,

Weepy, jolly however they be-
Goodbyes are very difficult for me...

9. To someone I admire..

May be words are not enough
To adorn your appreciation-crown,
Not perfect to portray every attribute
Still a try to pen it down...

Capturing every shade
Within your hazel eyes,
Words of pure magic
Elevating upto the skies.

Your most captivating smile
Say it all,
To be gentle on a succeeding turn
& to stay dauntless even after a fall!

Treasure of brains and beauty
Forming a classic blend,
Praising the virtues,erasing the vices
Setting a new trend.

You're an ideal personality
Perfect in every role,

Neither superficial nor perishable,
Its beauty of the soul !

10. Passing by the temple

As I pass by the temple
God, I want you to know the reason,
I would always be thankful
Regardless of the holy season..

'You' dont always plot a win-game
But does that really matter ?
Why should I be bothered when
I have so much on my platter !

Blessed with friends and fam
Without them its all tough,
How grand You have planned for me
I cant stress enough!

What all should I be grateful for
There's really too much to say,
Whenever a prayer crosses my mind
Its already sent on my way!

Not only You guard me physically
But care for my heart too,

When I get suddenly strong
God, I know its You!

I need to bow down to none
As long as I have 'thee',
I hope today you feel the love
Reflected back from me!

11. Monsoon calling!

The monsoon is back with rippling rain,
And those pants with soily stain.

Some stay inside for a cozy cuddle,
and some out in the muddy puddle.

Fritters are must for an instant snack,
They seem perfect with the cloudy-back

Half of them enjoy, half complain,
Some fall off the slippery terrain!

Remember the paperboats we left to sail,
Those should be for travel, instead of the rail!

The colorful umbrella-brigade on road,
Cheerfully greeting the frog and toad..

How can we forget the scented air,
All that comes from the wet-mud-affair

Many love rain, many of them dont,
When we wish to stop drizzle, surely it wont!

Somewhere its barren, elsewhere floody drains,
Who was ever perfect, to predict the moody rains!

12. All that deserves to be Re-thought.

Its not a good idea to point out on someone who turned skinny or chubby", they may be already concious about that.
If you do the same,
Rethink!

Many of them slept hungry in huts and others had a piece on the street.
If you feel life is unfair to you,
Rethink!

Givers give endlessly because takers dont have botherations of returning
If you are the one who only takes,
Rethink!

All that goes from you, comes around greater. God may forgive, but your actions wont.
If you ill-treat others,
Rethink!

There's always going to be someone who's above you and someone who's below.

If you compare and kill your vibe
Rethink!

Hardwork beats hardluck. No one finds more than they deserve.
If you think grass is greener elsewhere,
Rethink!

Pegions flock together, eagles dont!
If you're still trying to fit in the crowd,
Rethink!

Not everyone has to know your worth. There would be many who will hate you for no reason.
If you still give a damn,
Rethink!

Some often have complaints more than they have satisfactions.
If you are that complaint-box,
Rethink!

13. She

All she knew was to love with all her heart,
For her people she would even fall apart.

Poured her soul into everything,
Rhythms of bliss she'd all day sing.

She would possibly give all she could,
So hard she loved no one ever would.

Trying to heal others and make their day,
Praying for them when the days were grey.

She was all good, but always said sadly,
memories would make her miss days badly !

14. To the dads out there...

We notice your efforts and all that you do
And your concern, we appreciate that too!

We know, sometimes even you wish to be heard,
You endure body-aches without an upset-word!

You adjust so much without a second thought
And your pat on the back means alot!

For us, before you go on one more mile,
Get some break and rest for a while.

Dad, we never ever say it to you,
You're our strength, I hope you knew.

Without a pause, let us express this straight,
Before we realise that its too late..

You are the rescue to our heavy storm,
And equally dear to us, same as mom.

15. The old world charm

Today, my aged neighbours
Were flauting their old camera,
How happily they often express
Recollecting the vintage era!

We have surely heard the stories
Of walking on tedious miles,
Though it was a real struggle;
Grandpa tells it all with smiles!

Waiting for handwritten letters,
How could they keep calm ?!
Though phones made it better then,
But today we miss that charm...

No less than Pandora's box;
Is Granny's vintage trunk,
She has preserved her dear memories
Even if some call it junk!

Neither radios nor speakers
Only Gramophones used to sing,

That joy must be so different;
When Cinema was a rare thing!

Who thought that bell-bottoms;
Would hit back in fashion,
Fellows are still getting inn
For the retro styling-session.

I'm sure no one would exchange;
Their golden youth days,
For the life we live today;
And all our modern ways!

16. We at fault

Whenever we felt un-noticed,
It wasnt about the people around who ignored
It was us who seeked an approval.

Whenever we thought we lost our worth ,
It wasnt about the failed contest
It was us who attached self-worth to a mere competition.

Whenever we got hurt,
It wasnt about the careless ones
It was us who looked for the same kindness which we would rather show.

Whenever we felt people were unfair,
It wasnt about their disappointing behaviour
It was us who expected from wrong ones.

Whenever we felt mis-judged,
It wasnt about the judgemental ones
It was us who gave a damn to their opinions.

17. Educating the underprivileged

How can a family with nobody to earn-
Bearing the load of work and learn,
Encourage their child to write and read?
With no one to look after their basic need!

The food in mid break is often stuck
Coz how do they fill their empty stomach?
Though the school provides a meal for free,
But the womb that carried them is still hungry!

Getting them out through all this dark,
We have to gift them shine and spark!
Turning up their frowns to smiles,
Leading their way to fruitful miles..!

18. Nice to meet you ..

To the school teacher who praised for an art, rather than just the academic score
Nice to meet you!

To the active granny in highschool who believed in ageing gracefully, rather than just growing older
Nice to meet you!

To the lady who offered seat to a girl, rather than taking her young age for granted
Nice to meet you!

To the bus conductor, who cheerfully sung during his job rather than cribbing about the crowd
Nice to meet you!

To the boy who stopped and extended help for our punctured car, rather than getting on his own like all others did
Nice to meet you!

To the uncle who cared for a guy that fell over his bike, rather than cursing about his speed
Nice to meet you!

To all those who were selfless, Your kindness mattered alot.

Nice to meet ya'll !

Printed by Libri Plureos GmbH in Hamburg, Germany